At the Zoo

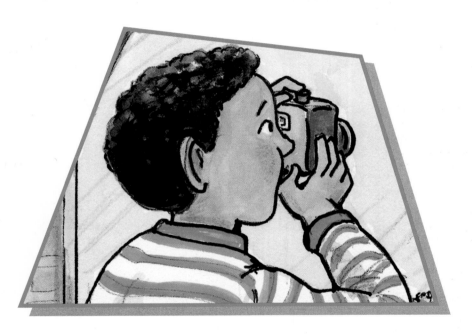

Written by Elizabeth Apgar

Illustrated by Cecile Schoberle

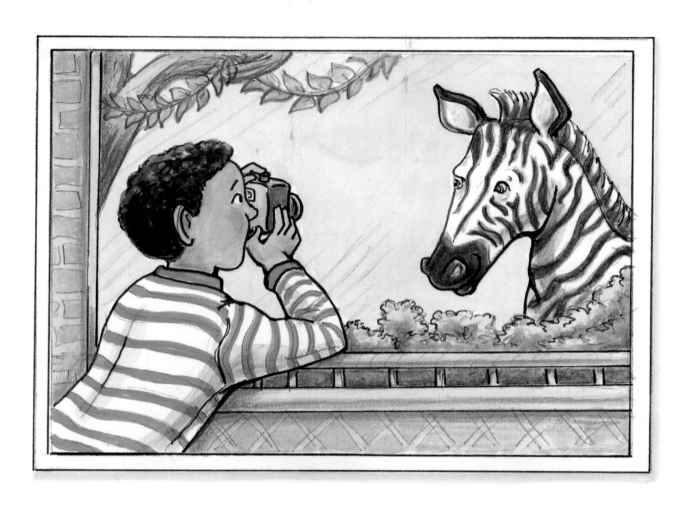

I saw a zebra at the zoo.

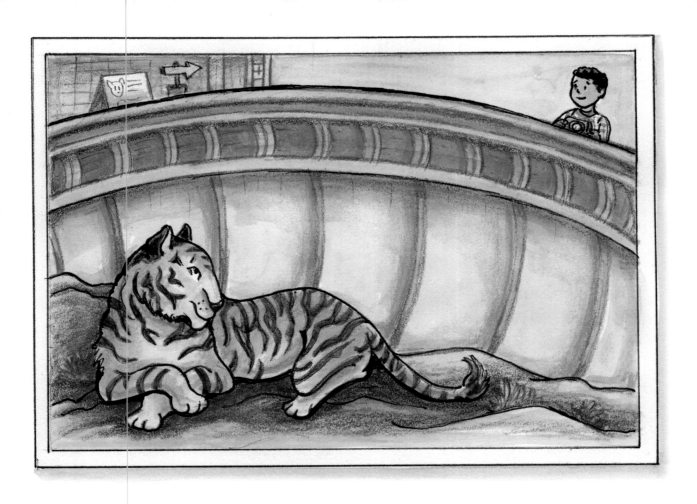

I saw a tiger at the zoo.

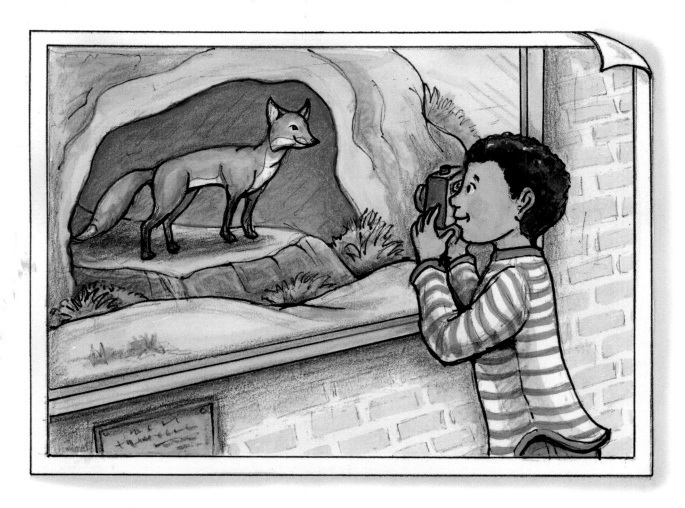

I saw a fox at the zoo.

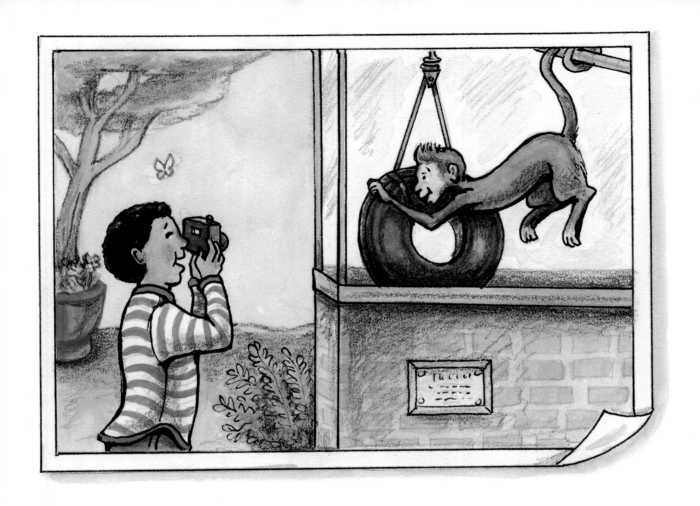

I saw a monkey at the zoo.

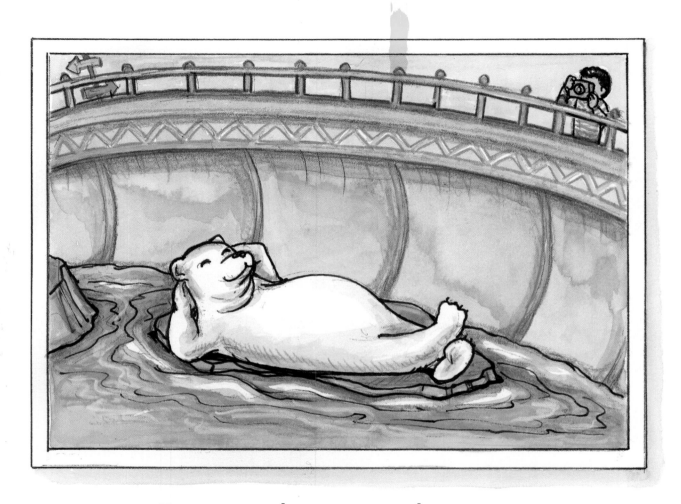

I saw a bear at the zoo.

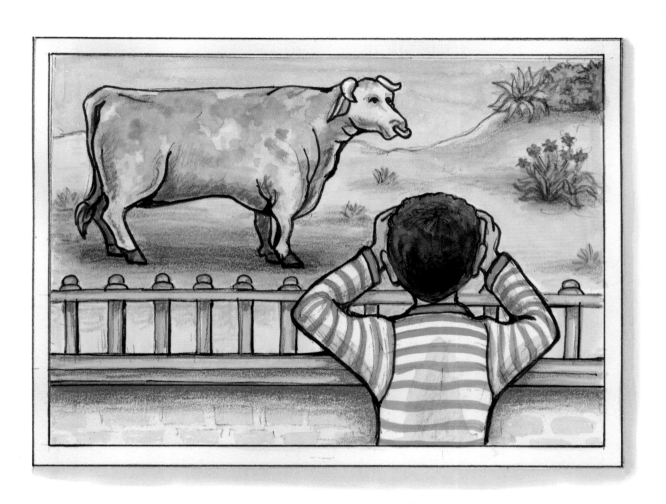

I saw an ox at the zoo.

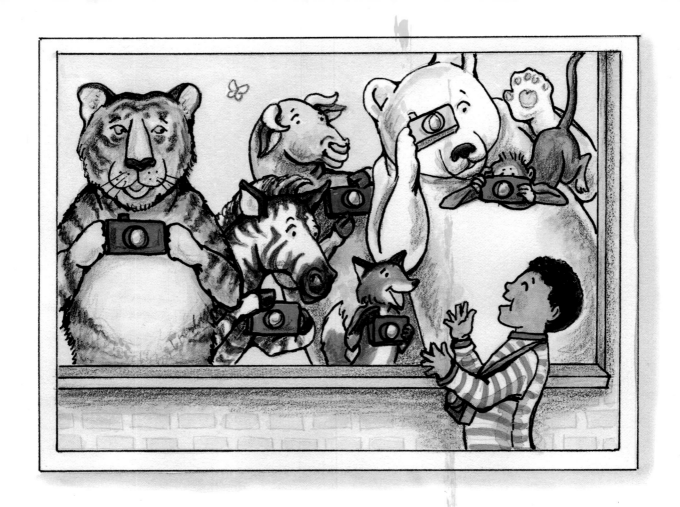

They saw me, too!